Student Athlete Success Guide

Maximize Your Potential

By

Karen W. Thompson

BK Royston Publishing
Jeffersonville, IN 47131
http://www.bkroystonpublishing.com
bkroystonpublishing@gmail.com

© Copyright – 2025

All Rights Reserved. No part of this book may be reproduced, stored in a retrieval system, or transmitted by any means without the written permission of the author.

Cover Design: Elite Covers

ISBN-13: 978-1-967282-62-3

Printed in the United States of America

Dedication

This book is dedicated to my granddaughters, Tiara and Madison, former AAU, high school, and college volleyball players—whose passion, perseverance, and character both on and off the court continue to inspire.

I also dedicate my book to all the families who remain steadfast in support of their student athletes everywhere. Your encouragement, sacrifices, and commitment help shape the lives of not only great players, but great people.

Table of Contents

Dedication   iii

Preface   ix

Introduction   xi

The Role of the Parents or the Guardians   1

What Is Civility?   3
◦Civility ◦Incivility ◦The Importance of Civility ◦Examples of Civility ◦How to Handle Civility ◦How to Handle Incivility

Sportsmanship   9
◦What Is the Difference Between Civility & Sportsmanship ◦Good Sportsmanship ◦Managing Unsportsmanlike Conduct ◦Social Settings

First Impressions   13
◦Hair Grooming ◦Face and Skin ◦Uniform Kit and Preparation ◦Posture and Stance ◦Teeth and Smile ◦Bright and Distracting Accessories ◦Body Language ◦Dress and Grooming ◦Communication Skills ◦Positive Attitude: In Interviews or Media Settings ◦Etiquette When Traveling ◦Making a Great First Impression ◦Do's and Don'ts: Banquets and Interviews

Communication in the Digital World   25
◦Advantages ◦Access to Resources ◦Communication & Networking ◦Performance Tracking◦ Disadvantages

◦Pressure to Maintain a Perfect Image ◦Distractions ◦Cyberbullying and Trolling ◦Privacy Risk ◦Unreliable Information ◦Etiquette Advice ◦Think Before Posting ◦Manage Privacy ◦ Use Social Media in a Positive Way ◦Healthy Screen Habits

Dynamics of Good Friendships   **31**
◦Be Supportive ◦Listen Actively ◦Celebrate Successes Together ◦Be Honest and Trustworthy ◦Show Empathy ◦Share Interest and Spend Time Together ◦Respect Boundaries and Differences ◦Apologize and Forgive ◦Include Others and Avoid Exclusion ◦Balance Sports and Personal Life

The Perils of Alcohol and Drugs   **37**
◦Understand the Risk ◦Recognize Peer Pressure ◦Set Personal Goals and Priorities ◦Surround Yourself with Positive Influences ◦Know How to Manage Temptation ◦Talk to Trustworthy Adults ◦Develop Coping Skills ◦Understand the Impact on Team and Reputation ◦Know the Consequences ◦Focus on Self-Care and Well-Being

Mental Health and Self-Care   **45**
◦Self-Care Tips ◦Resources: Crisis Text Line and National Alliance on Mental Illness (NAMI)

The Goal of Sports   **51**

Understanding Team Rules   **51**

Team Photo Shoot Preparation   **52**

Team Practice   **52**

Game Day Protocol   53

Celebrating a Championship   55

Table Manners   57
◦Before Meal ◦During Meal ◦After Meal ◦Informal Table-Setting

The End of the Season   63

Coaches Corner 1   65

Sharing First Impressions Tips with the Team   65
◦Lead By Example ◦Pre-Event Coaching ◦Role Playing

Team Building   67
◦Team Bonding Challenges ◦Team Workshops ◦Creative Sportsmanship Activities ◦Outdoor Adventures ◦Group Discussions and Reflections ◦Community Service Projects ◦Team Outings ◦ Skills and Drills That Promote Teamwork ◦Celebrating Success Together ◦Game Day Rituals

Coaches Corner 2   73

Promoting Civility in Student Athletes   73
◦Lead By Example ◦Encourage Open Communication ◦Acknowledge Good Behavior ◦Set Clear Expectations for Behavior ◦Foster a Culture of Empathy ◦Offer Conflict Resolution Training ◦Encourage Cooperation Over Competition ◦Create Inclusive Spaces

How to Manage Civility and Incivility in Student Athletes   75
◦Game Day Behavior ◦Encourage Emotional Regulation ◦Address Incivility Immediately ◦Promote Accountability ◦Use Consequences to Reinforce Expectations ◦Involve Parents in the Process ◦Example 1: Player Taunting after Scoring ◦Example 2: A Player Yells at a Teammate ◦Example 3: A Player Argues with the Referee 4: Player's Frustration At an Opponent ◦Example 5: Player Credit for a Team Effort

Post Game Interviews   85
◦Do's and Don'ts

Sharing Interview Etiquette with Team   89
◦Mock Interviews ◦Provide Role Model ◦Emphasize ◦"Team-First" Attitude

Code of Conduct Definitions   91

Resources   93

Afterword   95

About the Author   97

Preface

This book is not an exhaustive manual on all manners and etiquette rules, but rather a starting point to guide young student athletes through the important aspects of civility and behavior that will help them succeed in sports, school, and in life.

Civility goes beyond good manners, it shapes the way we interact with others, how we handle challenges, and how we treat ourselves. This book will provide useful guidelines for young student athletes, to stand out as an individual with great potential, both on and off the field.

Introduction

When you play sports, it's about more than just the physical ability, but it's about the teamwork, communication, and giving it your very best. But did you know that what you learn in school can help you become a better athlete? A strong academic foundation helps you develop the skills and mindset needed to succeed in sports as well. The more you learn, the better prepared you will be for challenges that arise both in school and in your athletic pursuits.

Think about your future. Doing well in school now will make it easier to balance academics and sports as you grow older. You're setting yourself up for success in both areas! Each day, you'll encounter decisions that will impact how you interact with people at home, at school, during practice, and even when traveling. As a young athlete, you'll need to be mindful of your choices, as they'll shape your relationships and your future. Manners are the tools that will help you navigate these situations successfully.

The Role of the Parents or the Guardians

Your parents or guardian are like your biggest fans and supporters. They help make sure you have a safe home to live in, food to eat, and clothes to wear. They work hard every day, sometimes taking on extra jobs or staying late at work, just so you can follow your dreams. One of those dreams might be cheerleading, baseball, basketball, football, lacrosse, soccer, track, volleyball or any other another sport! Parents pay for your fees, they drive you to practice, and they cheer for you at every game and competition.

But there's something else that's just as important as their love and support: showing appreciation for everything they do for you. It doesn't always have to be with big gestures; small acts of kindness can make a big difference. Imagine this: after a long day of school, completing homework assignments and practice, you decide to clean up your room, help with the dishes, or maybe even fold the laundry without being asked. These little actions can show your parents or guardian that you appreciate everything they do for you.

Being a good student is another way to show respect to your parents or guardian. When you turn in your homework on time, participate in class, and ask for help when you need it, you're not only becoming a better student, but you're also showing your parents that you value the education they're helping provide for you. Your parents or guardian work hard to give you these opportunities, so it's important to do your best and take responsibility for your schoolwork and actions.

What Is Civility?

Civility refers to the act of showing respect, kindness, and consideration for others, especially in interactions where there might be differences of opinion or tension. It involves treating people with dignity, maintaining politeness, and behaving in a way that fosters positive relationships and productive environments, whether in the workplace, at school, at home, or even in social settings.

Incivility, on the other hand, is the opposite. It refers to behaviors or attitudes that show a lack of respect, consideration, or regard for others. It includes actions, such as: rudeness, dismissiveness, or disrespecting the social norms and societal expectations for polite behavior. Incivility can lead to conflict, negativity, and a toxic atmosphere, whether in personal interactions or within large communities.

The Importance of Civility

Civility is essential because it fosters an environment where everyone feels valued and respected. It helps create strong relationships, both personal and professional, and it is the foundation for building trust. Whether you are playing a sport, learning in school, or interacting with family and friends, being civil allows you to manage challenges in a positive and a constructive way.

Examples of Civility:

1. **In School:**

    Civility: Students who listen to their classmates' perspectives, work cooperatively on group projects, and treat each other with kindness and empathy.

    Incivility: Bullying, mocking someone's appearance or ideas, or spreading rumors to undermine others.

2. **In Family Settings:**

    Civility: Respecting each other's boundaries, being polite during discussions, and compromising when disagreements arise.

    Incivility: Yelling, ignoring family members, or making hurtful comments during arguments.

3. **In Public Spaces:**

   Civility: Holding the door open for someone who is carrying bags or walking in behind you or politely asking someone to move if you need to pass through a crowded area Incivility: Shoving through crowds without regard for others or ignoring people in need of assistance.

4. **Social Media:**

   Civility: Engaging in thoughtful and respectful debate, even when opinions differ, and being mindful of the tone and language used.

   Incivility: Name-calling, personal attacks, or spreading false information to harm someone's reputation.

5. **At Work:**

   Civility: When a colleague disagrees with a proposal, they express their opinion respectfully, listening to others and offering constructive feedback without attacking or belittling others' ideas.

   Incivility: Interrupting colleagues during meetings, dismissing their ideas, or making sarcastic remarks.

How to Manage Incivility

Here are some ways to handle incivility and promote civility in different environments:

1. **Stay Calm and Composed:**
   When confronted with incivility, it is important to remain calm. Responding with anger or frustration can escalate the situation. Take a moment to breathe, and choose your response carefully.

2. **Address the Behavior Directly:**
   If you feel safe doing so, calmly and assertively address the behavior. For example, you can say, "I don't appreciate being spoken to that way," or "Let's discuss this respectfully." That sets a boundary without being confrontational.

3. **Avoid Engaging in a Tit-for-Tat Argument:**
   Responding to incivility with more incivility can quickly spiral into a negative interaction. Focus on maintaining your professionalism and your dignity, even if the other person does not.

4. **Set Clear Boundaries:**
   Let the other person know what behavior is unacceptable. For instance, if someone is being rude or dismissive, calmly explain you

expect a respectful dialogue and will not tolerate disrespectful behavior.

5. **Seek Mediation if Necessary:**
In cases where incivility escalates or does not resolve on its own, consider bringing in a neutral third party or mediator to help facilitate communication and resolve the issue.

6. **Document the Incidents:**
In workplace or school settings, if incivility persists, it might be helpful to document any incidents. That can be useful if further action needs to be taken, such as those involving a supervisor or a school administrator.

Sportsmanship

What Is the Difference Between Civility and Sportsmanship?

While civility is about respect and kindness in every aspect of life, sportsmanship specifically refers to how we behave in the context of sports. It includes playing fair, respecting your teammates and opponents, and handling victory or defeat with grace. Good sportsmanship builds respect and trust within the team and between competitors.

As a student athlete, you should handle sportsmanship with a blend of maturity and emotional intelligence. Respect for yourself and others, both on and off the field. Here are a few ways to navigate those situations:

Good Sportsmanship:

1. **Respect for Opponents and Teammates:** Show good sportsmanship by treating everyone, from teammates to opponents, with kindness and respect, regardless of the outcome of the game.

2. **Positive Communication:** Encourage open and respectful dialogue with teammates, coaches, and referees. Being polite and listening attentively helps build better relationships.

3. **Set an Example:** Athletes should act as role models, particularly for younger or newer players. Their behavior can set the tone for how others should behave.

4. **Acknowledging Effort:** Appreciate both individual and team efforts, no matter the score. Sports are not just about winning, but growing through experience.

Managing Unsportsmanlike Conduct:

1. **Stay Calm and Collected:** In the face of sportsmanship (whether it is trash talking, unsportsmanlike conduct, or rude behavior), it is important to stay calm. Reacting emotionally can escalate the situation. Focus on your game, not on the negativity.

2. **Avoid Retaliation:** Do not engage in insulting or hostile behavior. Responding to incivility with more incivility only fuels the negativity. Instead, focus on constructive ways to manage the situation.

3. **Seek Support from the Coach and/or the Team Staff:** If the situation becomes too difficult to manage on your own, talk to your coach or another trusted adult. They can help manage conflicts and provide guidance about how to navigate such issues in a mature way.

4. **Set Boundaries:** If someone crosses a line, it is okay to assertively express their behavior is not acceptable. Learning to advocate for yourself respectively is an important skill.

5. **Focus on the Bigger Picture:** Remember, the game of the day is temporary, but character and integrity last. Do not let temporary negative behaviors define you or distract you from your long-term goals.

Social Settings:

1. **Be Aware of Online Behavior:** In today's world, civility and sportsmanship extends to social media. You need to be respectful online: avoiding trolling, bullying, or posting negative comments about opponents, teammates, or coaches.

2. **Be Humble in Victory and Gracious in Defeat:** In social settings, you should understand the importance of humility, which entails celebrating wins with respect and handling losses with grace. That helps maintain good relationships in all areas of life.

3. **Support Others:** You can encourage and uplift your peers, and offer support in times of disappointment, fostering an environment of mutual respect. By maintaining composure, setting positive examples, and focusing on what is truly important (both in the game and beyond it), athletes can manage civility and incivility effectively and grow as people both on and off the field.

Do not scandalize your name, your family's name, or your school's name.

It is not worth it!

First Impressions

First impressions are incredibly important, especially at banquets, interviews, and when traveling with a team. First impressions shape how others perceive you and can set the tone for how you are treated, both immediately and long-term. Whether it is with a coach, an interviewer, a teammate, or even a fan, a positive first impression can open doors and create opportunities.

Here are some key tips on making a strong first impression, along with a few do's and don'ts:

1. **Hair Grooming:**

    Neat and Tidy: Make sure your hair is neat and well-groomed. That helps maintain a uniform look and ensures no one stands out for the wrong reasons.

    Haircuts: Get a haircut a few days before the team photo shoot or the game.

    Keep It Consistent: Team members with long hair, tie it back or keep it neat (e.g., ponytails, braids, or neat buns) to avoid stray hair falling in front of your faces.

2. **Face and Skin:**

   Shave or Groom Facial Hair: If you have facial hair, make sure your hair is groomed. Neatly trimmed beards or mustaches look better than messy, unkept facial hair.

   No Heavy Makeup (Unless Agreed Upon): If you wear makeup, it should be light and natural, focusing on enhancing their features and not distracting from them.

3. **Uniform Kit and Preparation:**

   Clean and Ironed Uniform Kit: Make sure your team's uniforms or jerseys are clean, free of wrinkles, and in good condition. A wrinkled or a stained uniform can detract from the overall look. Wear your uniform gear with confidence.

   Tidy Shoes: Ensure your shoes are clean and polished (especially for formal photos). Avoid scuff marks or dirt on shoes.

   Proper Fit: Clothes should fit properly, not too tight or too loose. Proper-fitting gear ensures everyone looks comfortable and confident.

4. **Posture and Stance:**

    Good Posture: Stand up straight with your shoulders back and your heads high. Good posture improves the overall appearance of the team and helps convey confidence.

    Avoid Slouching: Slouching or poor posture in a photo can make people look less engaged.

    Natural Stance: Stand naturally, without stiff poses. A slight angle (not facing the camera head-on) can often be more flattering.

    Hands: Position your hands naturally: either by your sides, resting on your hips, or gently holding the jersey. Avoid crossing arms or awkward hand positions.

5. **Teeth and Smile:**

    Fresh Breath: Brush your teeth before the photo or the game to avoid any lingering food smells.

    Smile Naturally: A natural smile is best. Relaxed and genuine expressions are key. Avoid too many teeth-whitening products. If using whitening products, it is best to keep it subtle. Overly white teeth can appear unnatural in photos.

6. **Bright or Distracting Accessories:**

   Make sure accessories are not too flashy or distracting. Simple, understated pieces work best in group photos.

   Hydration: Drink water beforehand. Hydrated skin looks better and more vibrant in photos.

7. **Body Language:**

   Stand Tall: Standing or sitting up straight shows you are engaged and present.

   Smile Genuinely: A friendly, warm smile helps put people at ease and conveys approachability.

   Eye Contact: Maintain steady, but natural, eye contact. Avoid staring down, as it can make you appear disengaged and insecure.

   Firm Handshake: (When Appropriate): A confident handshake can signal respect and professionalism. Make sure it is firm, but not overpowering. Avoid limp handshakes, which can give off an impression of disinterest.

Avoid Fidgeting: Excessive movement or nervous habits (like tapping your feet, adjusting your clothes constantly) can distract from your message and make you seem uncomfortable or unsure of yourself.

Mirroring: Subtly mirroring the other person's body language can make you seem more relatable and establish rapport.

8. **Dress and Grooming:**

   Dress for the Occasion: Whether it is for a banquet, an interview, or travel, dressing appropriately shows respect for the event and the people involved. Be sure your clothes are clean, well-fitted, and reflect the formality of the occasion.

   For Banquets: Even if the event is casual, avoid overly casual clothing, such as sweatpants or ripped jeans. A collared shirt or a neat jacket often works well.

   For Interviews: In a formal interview, wear something business casual or better. If it is a post-game interview, your uniform or team gear is the exception.

   Grooming is Key: A neat, polished appearance goes a long way. Make sure your hair is neat, your facial hair is well-groomed, and your nails are clean.

Avoid Overdoing It: Avoid heavy perfumes, colognes, or excessive jewelry, which can be distracting or seem unprofessional.

9. **Communication Skills:**

    Introduce Yourself Confidently: When meeting someone for the first time, introduce yourself clearly and confidently. "Hi, I'm [Your Name]; it's nice to meet you." If appropriate, offer a handshake as part of the greeting.

    Be Clear and Articulate: Speak clearly and at a moderate pace. Avoid speaking too quickly or mumbling, as it can make you seem unsure of yourself.

    Listen Actively: Show you are engaged by nodding, making eye contact, and responding thoughtfully. Avoid interrupting, and make sure you are fully present in the conversation.

    Be Mindful of Tone and Volume: A confident tone is essential. Speaking too quietly can make you seem unsure, while speaking too loudly can be off-putting. Be aware of your volume and speak with assurance.

Using Names: When addressing someone, using their name can help build rapport and shows attentiveness. For example, you can say, "Thank you, Coach [Last Name], for the opportunity."

10. Positive Attitude:

Be Friendly and Approachable: Make a conscious effort to be warm and approachable, especially when meeting new people or when in unfamiliar settings. A positive attitude will make people more comfortable around you.

Show Gratitude: When interacting with others, expressing gratitude, whether it is thanking someone for their time, their help, or for the opportunity to speak, can leave a lasting, positive impression.

Be Humble: Confidence is important, but humility is equally so. Acknowledging the efforts of others or showing appreciation for teamwork can make you seem more grounded and relatable.

11. Professionalism in Interviews or Media Settings:

Be Prepared: Whether it is a formal interview after a game or a casual media interaction, be prepared to speak about the game, your team, or your individual performance. Think through potential questions and answers beforehand.

Do Not Overdo It with Confidence: While it is important to protect confidence, avoid coming off as arrogant. Emphasize the collective team effort, and give credit where it is due.

Keep It Positive: Even if the game did not go as planned, maintain a positive outlook. Avoid saying anything negative about your teammates, your coaches, or the competition.

Be Respectful: Respect the interviewer's time, and make sure to thank them at the end. Be courteous and professional, whether you have had a good game or a bad one.

12. Etiquette When Traveling:

Be Punctual: Being on time (or early) is one of the simplest, yet most effective, ways to make a good first impression. It shows you value others' time and are dependable.

Be Respectful of Others: Whether it is in a hotel, on a bus, or in a new city, remember you are a representative of your team and your organization. Respect your teammates, your coaches, and the people you encounter during travel.

Stay Organized: Have your personal items (like your uniform, your travel documents, or your gear) organized and ready. Disorganization can make you appear scattered and unprepared.

Avoid Disruptive Behavior: Do not engage in loud, disruptive, or inappropriate behavior when traveling. Keep noise levels to a minimum, respect public spaces, and avoid drawing unwanted attention to yourself.

13. Making a Great First Impression:

Be Genuine: People can usually tell when someone is being fake or disingenuous. Be yourself. Authenticity is always more impressive than trying too hard to fit in or be someone you are not.

Take Initiative: Offering help, asking questions, or showing interest in others can set you apart as proactive and engaged. Do not wait for things to come to you; take the lead.

Show Respect for Others: Treat everyone with kindness and respect, whether it is your coach, a teammate, or someone whom you have just met.

14. Do's and Don'ts for First Impressions at Banquets and Interviews:

Do's:

Be punctual to show your respect for the time of others.

Smile and use positive body language to appear approachable.

Greet others politely with a firm handshake and a friendly introduction.

Make eye contact and listen attentively to the conversation.

Be gracious and thank others for their time and their hospitality.

Be ready to share your purpose in life, your career aspirations, and your plans for the next five years.

Follow through with any commitments you make (whether in a team meeting or interview).

Don'ts:

Don't interrupt others when they are speaking, and avoid dominating the conversation.

Don't complain or focus on negative topics, especially when meeting someone new or speaking during an interview.

Don't be late or show up unprepared. That reflects poorly on your professionalism.

Don't fidget or appear distracted during conversations or interviews.

Don't be too informal. Keep the tone respectful and appropriate for the occasion.

Don't monopolize the conversation or talk too much about yourself.

By focusing on making a positive first impression, athletes not only enhance their personal image, but also contribute to the overall success and professionalism of the team.

Communication in a Digital World

Technology plays a large role in our lives today. It is important to remember the same principles of civility apply online as they do offline. In this section, we will discuss digital etiquette, how to communicate effectively online, and the importance of tone, vocabulary, and being respectful in digital spaces.

Growing up in a digital world has numerous advantages, but you can also face several challenges. Here is a breakdown of key points:

Advantages:

1. **Access to Resources:**

    Training Materials: They can help you easily access instructional videos, workout routines, nutritional advice, and professional athlete insights.

    Expert Guidance: At the proper time, you can connect directly with coaches, fitness experts, and even sports psychologists on digital platforms.

    Motivation and Community: Social media allows you to follow other athletes, participate in virtual challenges, and get inspired by global peers.

Visibility and Branding: Digital platforms help you build personal brands, potentially leading to sponsorships and exposure at an early age.

2. **Communication and Networking:**

   Team Collaboration: Digital tools like Slack, Zoom, or even WhatsApp groups help teams stay connected, plan strategies, or discuss the game while apart.

   Global Networking: You can connect with other young talents globally, exchanging tips and experiences, and learning from different cultures or playing styles.

3. **Performance Tracking:** There are many apps and wearables (e.g., Fitbit, Strava) to track progress, monitor health, and analyze training data, helping you optimize your performance.

4. **Mental Health Support:** Digital platforms provide access to mental health resources and communities where athletes can talk about performance anxiety, their stress, or other mental struggles they face during their careers.

Challenges:

1. **Pressure to Maintain a Perfect Image:** Social media platforms create an environment where you feel pressure to show perfection whether in your appearance, your achievements, or your lifestyle. That can lead to mental health issues, such as anxiety, depression, and body image concerns.

2. **Distractions:** The ease of accessing entertainment, social media, and other distractions can impact your focus on training and academics, leading to procrastination and time mismanagement.

3. **Cyberbullying and Trolling:** Athletes, especially younger ones, are prone to negative comments, hate messages, and pressure from strangers or fans. That can severely impact your self-esteem.

4. **Privacy Risk:** Sharing too much personal information online can put you at risk of identity theft, stalking, or other privacy violations. There is also the risk of oversharing moments of frustration or failure that can harm your reputation.

5. **Unreliable Information:**
   The digital world is filled with both good and bad advice. You can be misled by unqualified influencers or scams promising quick results in training, which can lead to injury or setbacks.

Etiquette Advice for Athletes in the Digital World:

1. **Think Before Posting:**
   Always consider how a post, an image, or a video might be perceived by others. While it is tempting to share everything, it is essential to think about the long-term impact on your reputation, your teammates, or your sponsors. Avoid posting during moments of frustration, anger, or disappointment. Negative emotions can be misinterpreted and might leave a digital trail.

2. **Respect Others:**
   Be mindful of the language and the tone you use in comments, direct messages, or posts. It is easy to engage in trash talk, but a professional attitude helps you maintain respect among peers and fans. Support others by celebrating their wins, sharing encouraging words, and being kind.

3. **Manage Your Privacy:**
   Protect your personal information. Review your social media privacy settings to limit who can view your posts. That can help safeguard against unwanted attention. Be cautious about sharing your location data or any other sensitive details that can compromise your safety.

4. **Use Social Media in a Positive Way:**
   Use platforms to inspire, educate, and connect with your audience. Share your journey, your setbacks, and your triumphs, and try to uplift others during the process. Avoid engaging in online arguments or in petty drama. It is better to stay out of controversial situations that can harm your reputation.

5. **Healthy Screen Habits:**
   While digital tools can enhance your career, it is essential to also focus on face-to-face interactions with coaches, teammates, and mentors. Make sure you take breaks from screens to recharge mentally and physically, ensuring your life off the phone supports your overall well-being.

By navigating the digital space with a clear sense of responsibility and professionalism, you can take advantage of the opportunities that online communities provide and minimize risk.

Dynamics of Good Friendships

A good friendship is based on trust, communication, and mutual respect. Learn how to build and maintain healthy friendships, both on and off the field. Are you the type of person you would want as a friend? Being a good friend is an important skill for you to develop. The values you can learn in sports, such as teamwork, respect, and support are directly applicable to friendships and can help you build strong, lasting relationships.

Here are some ways you can be good friends:

1. **Be Supportive:**

    Encourage Your Friends: Just like teammates, friends appreciate support during both good times and bad times. Whether it is cheering on a friend during the big game, helping them through a tough time, or just being there when they need you, showing support strengthens friendships.

    Example: You attend your friend's recital or academic event, showing interest and enthusiasm for their achievements outside of sports.

2. **Listen Actively:**

   Be a Good Listener: Sometimes, being a good friend means simply being present and listening. Let your friends talk about their feelings, their concerns, or their experiences without interrupting or offering advice, unless they ask for it. Listening makes your friends feel valued and understood.

   Example: After a challenging day, your friend might talk about feeling frustrated with their performance in sports or in school. Instead of offering quick solutions, just listen and empathize with them.

3. **Celebrate Successes Together:**

   Be Happy for Your Friends: When a friend achieves something, whether it is winning a match or making progress on personal goal, celebrate their success! It is important to show you are genuinely happy for them, not jealous or competitive.

   Example: You cheer for a friend who wins an award or hits a personal milestone. Instead of focusing on your own accomplishments, you acknowledge and celebrate your friend's victory with enthusiasm.

4. **Be Honest and Trustworthy:**

    Build Trust Through Honesty: Good friendships are built on trust. Being honest about your feelings, your opinions, and your actions is vital. If something is bothering you, it is okay to have a respectful conversation about it. Being dependable and trustworthy makes you a reliable friend.

    Example: If a friend asks for your opinion about a decision they are making, give them an honest and a thoughtful answer, but also do so in a way that is respectful and caring.

5. **Show Empathy and Compassion:**

    Understand and Care for Your Friend's Emotions: Empathy is about putting yourself in your friend's shoes and showing you care about their feelings. Sometimes, being a good friend means comforting them during tough moments, even if you do not have all the answers.

    Example: If a friend is feeling down because of a loss in a game or personal challenge, offer words of encouragement. Let them know you understand their frustration, and remind them setbacks are part of the journey.

6. **Share Interests and Spend Time Together:**

   Spend Quality Time Together: Make an effort to hang out with your friends outside of sports. Shared experiences outside a competitive setting can strengthen your bond. Participate in activities both of you enjoy, even if they are not related to sports.

   Example: After a long season of training, a group of friends decides to have a movie night, go for a hike, or simply hang out and talk. Those fun moments help friendships grow stronger.

7. **Respect Boundaries and Differences:**

   Understand Individual Needs and Limits: Every friend has different preferences, interests, and limits. Respecting those differences is a key part of being a good friend. If a friend needs space or time to themselves, acknowledge that without taking it personally.

   Example: If a friend is not feeling up for hanging out or talking, respect their need for space, and do not pressure them. A true friend understands sometimes people need to recharge.

8. **Apologize and Forgive:**

    Take Responsibility and Make Amends: No friendship is perfect, and sometimes misunderstandings or mistakes happen. Being a good friend means apologizing when you have hurt someone and forgiving them after they've made a mistake. Learn from the experience and move on.

    Example: If you unintentionally hurt a friend's feelings whether during a game or during a conversation, take the time to apologize sincerely. Also, forgive them when they make mistakes or say something wrong.

9. **Include Others and Avoid Exclusion:**

    Be Inclusive and Kind: A good friend does not leave others out. You can be especially mindful about how you include others, making sure no one feels left out, whether it is in social settings or on the team.

    Example: If you notice one of your friends sitting alone during a practice or team hangout, invite them to join the group, ensuring everyone feels welcome.

10. Balance Sports and Personal Life:

Respect Your Friend's Other Interests: While sports are important, it is also important to remember your friends have other interests. Encourage your friends to pursue their passions outside sports and be supportive of their goals, whether in academics, in hobbies, or in other areas.

Example: You can support your friends in pursuing other interests, such as art or music lessons. Show genuine interest in your friend's non-sporting passions and celebrate those achievements, as well.

In Summary: Being a good friend as a student athlete involves practicing kindness, empathy, respect, and active support qualities that overlap with being a good teammate. The lessons you learn on the field, such as working together, handling success and failure, and treating others with respect, can all help foster strong supportive friendships. By developing those qualities, both in and out of sports, athletes can cultivate lasting friendships that enrich their lives throughout adulthood.

The Perils of Alcohol and Drugs

As a student athlete, it is essential you understand the dangers of alcohol, drugs, and vaping. Those substances can have a negative impact on your physical and mental well-being, harming your reputation, your athletic performance, and your overall health. They can also impair your decision-making, slow your reflexes, and increase the risk of injury. Moreover, substances can interfere with your training, making it harder to reach your goals. Choosing to avoid those substances not only helps you perform better, but also shows respect for family, yourself, your teammates, and your sport. Staying away from alcohol, drugs, and vaping is an important part of maintaining your health, staying focused, and achieving success in all areas of life.

Making healthy choices about alcohol, drugs, vaping, and other risky behaviors is crucial and can directly impact your performance, your health, and your overall well-being.

Here are some strategies and considerations for staying away from substances:

1. **Understand the Risk:**

    Educate Yourself: Knowledge is power. It is important for you to understand the harmful effects of alcohol, drugs, and vaping. Those substances can negatively affect physical health (e.g., lung and heart function, muscle recovery) and mental health (e.g., mood swings, depression, anxiety). Additionally, they can impact your focus, your endurance, and your ability to perform.

Example: Understand alcohol can disrupt sleep patterns and slow recovery after training.

2. **Recognize Peer Pressure:**

   Be Confident in Saying "No": Peer pressure can be a major factor as to why some young athletes experiment with substances. It is important to build confidence in your ability to say "No" without feeling guilty or pressured to conform. That can be easier if you already have a keen sense of self and their priorities.

   Example: When offered a vape by a peer, politely refuse by saying something like, "I need to stay in shape for my game," or "It's not for me."

3. **Set Personal Goals and Priorities:**

   Stay Focused on Your Goals: For many athletes, their dreams involve reaching higher levels of competition, earning scholarships, or even turning pro. Keeping those long-term goals in mind can help you make better choices in the moment.

Example: You are a high school runner who dreams of making the varsity team will. You also understand drinking alcohol or using drugs can harm your speed, your recovery, and your endurance. That can motivate you to stick to healthier habits.

4. **Surround Yourself with Positive Influences:**

   Choose Supportive Friends: The people you surround yourself with have a major influence on your decisions. Being around friends who value health, sportsmanship, and making good choices can help reinforce positive behavior. Likewise, seeking out mentors, coaches, and teammates who live healthy lifestyles can encourage you to follow suit.

   Example: You might find strength in a supportive group of teammates who do not drink or use substances. That positive peer group can influence you to stay away from unhealthy habits and focus on what is best for your athletic performance.

5. **Know How to Manage Temptation:**

   Have a Plan: Knowing ahead of time how to manage situations where alcohol, drugs, or vaping might be present can be empowering. Whether it is a party, a social gathering, or a peer offering you something, being prepared with a response or a way to exit the situation can help you avoid making a poor decision.

Example: If a group of friends is going out to a party where drinking is involved, you might plan to stay home or offer to hang out somewhere else, knowing that is better for your health and your goals.

6. **Talk to Trustworthy Adults:**

    Seek Guidance: Parents, coaches, and other trustworthy adults can offer valuable advice about how to avoid risky behaviors. They can help you navigate the pressures they face, offer insight into the long-term effects of substance use, and help them make decisions aligned with their values.

    Examples: If you feel unsure or conflicted about peer pressure or a specific situation, talking to a coach or a parent who understands your goals can provide clarity and reassurance about making the right decision.

7. **Develop Coping Skills:**

    Healthy Approach to Handling Stress and Emotions: Sports often come with pressures, and learning how to deal with stress and emotions in healthy ways can reduce the temptation to turn to substances for coping. You should focus on stress-management techniques like deep breathing, journaling, talking with your friends, or engaging in other hobbies you enjoy.

Example: Instead of using substances to manage the stress of a big game or a difficult practice, you can go for a run or talk with a teammate to relieve stress and stay calm.

8. **Understand the Impact on Team & Reputation:**

    Be a Role Model: You should often look up to your peers, as they also set an example for others. Being mindful of the message you send about making healthy choices can impact your teammates and younger athletes. Being a positive role model not only helps you stay accountable, but also reinforces the importance of making good choices in the eyes of others.

    Examples: A captain of the soccer team who maintains a drug-free lifestyle can set a powerful example for younger players. Their actions can inspire others to make similar choices and prioritize their health and goals.

9. **Know the Consequences:**

   Be Aware of Penalties and Consequences: Many sports have strict rules about substance use, and breaking those rules can result in suspensions, bans, or loss of eligibility. Understanding those consequences can reinforce the importance of staying drug and alcohol free.

   Example: You know using drugs can lead to losing a scholarship or getting banned from a competition, so you will be less likely to risk your future for temporary satisfaction.

10. **Focus on Self-Care and Well-Being:**

    Prioritize Health: Understanding taking care of your body is an essential part of being a successful athlete. Healthy habits, such as eating well, getting enough sleep, staying hydrated, and exercising regularly are all part of an integrated approach to performance. Avoiding substances that can harm your body is part of that commitment to self-care.

    Example: Prioritize getting eight hours of sleep before a big competition, knowing sleep is crucial for peak performance. Seek professional mental health support when you need help.

In Summary: By understanding the risks, setting goals, surrounding yourself with positive influences, and practicing good decision-making, you can stay focused on your health and your success. The ability to make healthy choices about staying away from alcohol, drugs, and vaping comes down to staying true to your values, being confident in saying "No," and always remembering the bigger picture: a bright future in sports and beyond.

Mental Health and Self-Care

Mental health is just as important as physical health, especially for athletes who often face pressures both in sports and in daily life. Taking care of your mental well-being involves managing stress, maintaining a positive attitude, and reaching out for help when you need it. Practicing self-care can include activities like taking time to relax, talking to parents or a trusted adult or counselor about your feelings, and finding ways to stay calm during stressful situations. Just as you rest your body after practice, it is also vital to give your mind the care it needs. Taking care of your mental health ensures you stay balanced, focused, and able to perform your best in all aspects of life.

Self-Care Tips:

- Schedule time for self-care.
- Give your parents or guardians a hug.
- Spend time with family.
- Cook and eat healthy meals at home.
- Get proper rest.
- Take a break from technology.
- Employ deep breathing techniques.
- Go for a walk and enjoy nature's beauty.
- Embrace any hobbies you enjoy.
- Focus on your educational career.
- Reflect on your individual goals.
- Read an inspiring biography.
- Recite daily your personal mantra.
- Journal your accomplishments.

What would you like to add to your list?

_____

_____

_____

List your top five self-care favorites:

_____

_____

_____

_____

_____

Write down your accomplishments.

_____

_____

_____

_____

What do you consider to be failures or setbacks?

_____

_____

_____

_____

What did you learn from the detours of your failures or your setbacks?

_____

_____

_____

_____

How did the experience affect your confidence?

_____
_____
_____
_____
_____
_____
_____
_____
_____
_____
_____
_____
_____
_____
_____
_____
_____

Remember, you are not alone!

Help is available.

Talk to your parents or guardians.

Get professional counseling if you need it.

Need to vent?

Resources:

Crisis Text Line:

https://www.crisistextline.org

Text Home to 741741

National Alliance on Mental Illness (NAMI):

https://www.nami.org

Call or text 988 or chat 988lifeline.org

The Goal of Sports

The goal of sports is not just about winning; it is also about being part of a team, improving your skills, and learning valuable life lessons. Sports help teach discipline, teamwork, resilience, and perseverance. Whether it is through overcoming challenges, celebrating victories, or learning from defeats, sports will teach you how to manage both success and failure with grace. Being part of a team teaches you how to collaborate, communicate, and work toward a common goal. Sports are an excellent way to develop physical fitness, build character, and make lifelong friends.

Understanding Team Rules

The coach will share team rules. Every team has specific rules that help ensure fairness, respect, and discipline. Those rules are essential for creating a positive environment where everyone can succeed. They are designed to help ensure everyone works together to achieve success. Team rules cover everything from being on time for practice to showing respect for teammates and coaches. Following those rules helps build discipline, promotes a positive atmosphere, and allows the team to function smoothly. As a student athlete, it is important you understand and adhere to those guidelines because they reflect your commitment to the team and contribute to the overall success of the group. Respecting team rules is a key part of being a responsible athlete.

Team Photo Shoot Preparation

Team photo shoots are a wonderful way to capture memories and commemorate your athletic journey. To ensure the best results, it is important to properly prepare. Start by grooming yourself; make sure your hair is neat, your face is clean, and your uniform is in good condition. Pay attention to details, such as posture and stance, as standing tall with a confident smile helps create a positive image. Remember, it is an opportunity to highlight your team spirit and pride, so bring your best attitude to the shoot.

Team Practice

Practice is where you develop your skills and improve as a player. Learn how to make the most of your practice sessions and strengthen your abilities. It is important to approach practice with a positive attitude, a strong work ethic, and a willingness to improve. That is your time to learn, to grow, and to make mistakes in a safe environment, so do not be afraid to challenge yourself. Focus on developing your individual skills while also being mindful of how your actions impact the team. Practicing with effort and enthusiasm not only helps you improve as a student athlete, but also encourages your teammates to do the same. Consistent practice leads to success, so make the most of every session.

Game Day Protocol

Game day is both an exciting and a nerve-wracking experience for every student athlete. There are certain protocols you should follow to ensure you are ready to perform at your best. Those include arriving early, warming up, showing respect for opponents, and handling victory and defeat with grace. Approach game day with a focused and a calm mindset. Arrive early to ensure you have time to warm up and mentally prepare for the game. Be attentive to the National Anthem, and always show respect for the visiting team, regardless of the game's outcome. Whether you are starting or coming off the bench, always play your best and contribute to the team in any way you can. After the game, win or lose, be kind and congratulate your opponents. Following proper game day protocol helps you maintain professionalism and ensures everyone enjoys the experience.

Celebrating a Championship

When your team wins a championship, it is important to celebrate your success while remaining humble. Learn how to manage your success with grace and appreciation.

Winning a championship is a major and significant achievement, but it is important to celebrate with humility. While it is natural to feel excited and proud of your hard work, remember sportsmanship means showing respect to all involved, including your opponents. Celebrate your success with your teammates, but avoid boasting or gloating. Staying humble after a victory allows you to appreciate the journey, the teamwork, and the effort that led to the win. It is also a reminder success is temporary, and humility helps keep you grounded as you continue to grow and improve as an athlete. So, stay humble.

Table Manners

Etiquette and table manners are important for creating a respectful and an enjoyable dining experience for everyone. When sitting down to a meal, it is essential to remember basic table manners, such as waiting for everyone to be served before beginning to eat, chewing with your mouth closed, and engaging in polite conversation. Keep your elbows off the table, and be mindful of your posture. When it comes to place settings, understanding the proper arrangements of utensils and glassware can make a significant difference. Typically, utensils are arranged in the order they will be used, with those for the first course on the outside and those for the main course closer to the plate. Forks are placed to the left of the plate, knives and spoons to the right, with the knife blade facing the plate. Glassware should be positioned above the knife, and a napkin is often placed on the left or on the plate. Knowing those basic table settings and practicing good manners ensures a positive dining experience and shows respect for others.

1. **Before the Meal:**

    • Be on Time: Arrive early, or on time. Being punctual shows respect for the event and for others' time.

- Wait for the Host: Wait until everyone is served and for the host or the coach to begin eating before you start. That is a sign of respect.

- Sit Properly: Sit up straight with feet flat on the floor. Do not slouch or lean too far back in your chair.

- Napkin Etiquette: As soon as you sit down, place your napkin on your lap. If you leave the table temporarily, leave the napkin on your chair, not on the table.

2. **During the Meal:**

    - Chew with Your Mouth Closed: That is one of the most important table manners to remember. No one wants to see food in your mouth.

    - Use the Correct Utensils: Start with the utensils farthest from your plate and work your way in. For example, the outermost fork is typically for salads, the next one is for the main course, etc.

    - Cut Small Bites: Cut your food into manageable pieces to avoid large bites.

    - Keep Your Elbows off the Table: Keep your elbows by your sides or on your lap when you are not using your utensils.

- Engage in Conversation: Participate in polite, light conversation with others at the table. Avoid discussing negative or controversial topics.

- Be Considerate with Your Voice: Speak in a polite, moderate tone, without shouting or talking too loudly. Avoid talking with your mouth full.

- Pass Food Correctly: Pass food to the right. If someone asks for something, pass the item to them directly rather than pointing or grabbing it for them.

- Wait for Desert: Do not rush through the meal. Wait for the course to be finished before moving on to dessert or coffee.

3. **After the Meal:**

- Do not Rush: Take your time finishing the meal. When you are finished, place your utensils parallel on the plate, with the tines of the fork facing up.

- Thank the Host: Always express gratitude to the host or the coach for the meal, whether it is a formal banquet or a casual dinner.

- Be Discreet with Complaints: If there is a problem with the food or the service, address it privately and calmly rather than making a scene.

Informal Place Setting Illustration

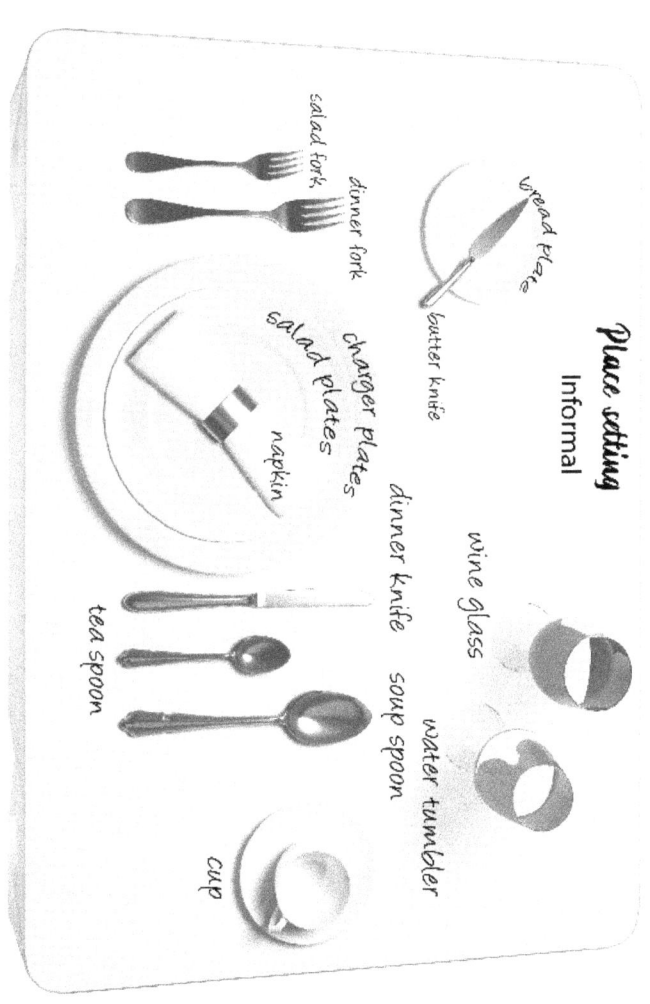

The End of the Season

The end of the season is a time for reflection, celebration, and recognition. This section covers the typical events that take place during the end-of-season, such as banquets or award ceremonies.

Those provide an opportunity to reflect on the season's accomplishments, recognize individual achievements, and celebrate team successes. It is time to show appreciation for teammates, coaches, and parents who contributed to the season's success. Those events often include speeches, awards, and social time, allowing players to bond and create lasting memories. As the season concludes, it is important to express gratitude for the experience and look forward to future opportunities for growth and improvement.

Coaches Corner 1

Sharing First Impression Tips with the Team

Coaching a team requires dedication, perseverance, and a genuine passion for helping others succeed. It is not just about strategy and skills, but also about building trust, motivating players, and fostering a positive environment. If you aspire to become a coach one day, it is important to understand the challenges and rewards that come with the role. To give you a better insight into what coaching a team truly entails, I have added Coaches Corner 1 and 2.

The Coaches Corner sections will give you an idea about what it is like to coach a team. An athlete might have an opportunity to be a part-time coaching assistant during the summer or participate in various local skills camps or sports clinics for young athletes.

• Lead By Example: As a coach, show how to make a good first impression through your own behavior. Be on time, dress appropriately, and engage with others in a respectful manner.

• Pre-Event Coaching: Before a banquet, an interview, or a trip, remind the team of the importance of first impressions. Go over simple rules like "Be on time," "Be respectful," and "Always show appreciation."

- Role-Playing: During practice sessions, practice introductions or interview scenarios will help athletes feel confident and prepared for when the real moment comes.

Team Building

Building a strong, cohesive team is essential for success. This section includes ideas for specific team-building activities that have the ability to strengthen communication, trust, and respect.

Team-building activities are essential for fostering a sense of unity and collaboration among athletes. Those activities help athletes build trust, improve communication, and strengthen relationships both on and off the field. Team-building exercises can range from simple icebreakers to more complex challenges that require teamwork to solve. Engaging in such activities help athletes bond and develop a dedicated team dynamic, which is crucial for success in sports. Whether it is participating in group discussions, team outings, or community service projects, those experiences help athletes work together and support each other, fostering an environment of respect and teamwork. Creating a bonding activity for student athletes is a wonderful way to foster teamwork, communication, and respect key elements of good sportsmanship.

Here are some activity ideas to strengthen relationships, build trust, and promote positive team dynamics:

1. **Team-Bonding Challenges:**

• Human Knot: Have team members stand in a circle, grab hands with two different people across from them, and try to untangle themselves without letting go of the others' hands.

• Relay Race with a Twist: Create relay races during which team members must work together in some way beyond just running, such as passing a ball in unique ways during the race or solving puzzles together.

2. **Team Workshops:**

• "Who Am I?" Icebreaker: Each team member writes down one thing about themselves (something unique but not obvious), and the rest of the team must guess who it belongs to. That promotes understanding and helps players learn about each other's interests and backgrounds.

• Goal Setting Session: Have team members work together to set individual and team goals for the season. Discuss how to support each other in achieving those goals, and create a collective team goal to work toward.

3. **Creative Sportsmanship Activities:**

• Compliment Circle: Have the team stand in a circle, and each player gives a compliment to the person standing next to them. The compliments can be about skills, attitude, effort, or anything positive related to sportsmanship.

• Sportsmanship Role Play: Create scenarios during which team members must act out good (and poor) sportsmanship. Discuss how they would manage those situations in real life and what actions reflect positive sportsmanship.

4. **Outdoor Adventures:**

• Scavenger Hunt: Organize a sports-themed scavenger hunt during which the team members must work together to find clues and complete challenges.

• Obstacle Course: Set up a physical or a mental obstacle course where teamwork is essential to complete tasks, whether it is balancing a ball, solving a puzzle, or working in pairs.

• Hiking or Nature Walk: Take the team on a short hike or a nature walk, encouraging informal conversation. Nature is a great setting for relaxing and connecting.

5. **Group Discussions and Reflection:**

• Team Reflection Journals: After games or practices, have athletes write in a journal or discuss what went well, what could be improved, and how they can support one another moving forward.

• Sportsmanship Reflection Circle: After a game or a practice, sit in a circle and share one thing each person did that showed good sportsmanship, whether that was helping a teammate, encouraging someone, or staying calm in the face of adversity.

6. **Community Service Projects:**

• Volunteering Together: Organize a community service event during which the team volunteers together, such as cleaning up a local park, helping at a food bank, or organizing a charity event. Working toward a common cause can strengthen team bonds and emphasize the importance of giving back.

• Charity Games: Host a "friendly" sports game or tournament, where players play for a charitable cause, promoting the idea sports can have a positive impact beyond the field.

7. **Team Outings or Socials:**

• Movie Night: Watch a sports movie together, followed by a discussion about the lessons learned from the characters' teamwork, perseverance, and sportsmanship.

- Picnic or BBQ: Hold a casual picnic or a BBQ during which team members can relax and socialize outside of the competitive environment, helping to build friendships in a fun, low-pressure setting.

- Bowling or Mini Golf: Plan a team outing to a bowling alley or a mini-golf course. Friendly competition in a non-sport setting helps team members bond and learn to interact outside a strict team structure.

8. **Skills & Drills That Promote Teamwork:**

- Two-Partner Skill Drills: Have players pair up and practice skills together, such as passing, shooting, or dribbling, depending on the sport. Encourage them to give each other feedback and support.

- Team Skills Challenge: Create a set of skill-based challenges during which the team must work together to complete them. That can include passing drills, relay races, or agility courses that require communication and collaboration.

9. **Celebrating Success Together:**

- End-of-the-Season Celebration: Host a team party or a gathering to celebrate the season's achievements, big or small. That can include distributing awards for things like "Best Sportsmanship," "Hardest Worker," and "Most Improved."

• Shout-out Wall: Create a team "shout-out" wall or a board on which teammates can leave positive notes for each other throughout the season. That can be a physical space or on a digital platform.

10. **Game Day Rituals:**

• Pre-Game Huddle or Chant: Develop a team chant or a ritual athletes perform to create a sense of unity before each game. That can be a motivational chant, a cheer, or a team handshake.

• Post-Game High Five Line: After games, have players line up and give each other high-fives or handshakes as a team, reinforcing camaraderie and mutual respect regardless of the game's outcome.

Coaches Corner 2

Promoting Civility in Student Athletes

1. **Lead by Example:**

• Show kindness, patience, and respect in your daily interactions. When others see you modeling those behaviors, they are more likely to follow suit.

2. **Encourage Open Communication:**

• Create an environment in which people feel safe to express their thoughts and their opinions. Encourage listening and understanding, not responding.

3. **Acknowledge Good Behavior:**

• Recognize and praise acts of civility. Positive reinforcement can motivate others to act similarly. For example, acknowledging a colleague's respectful behavior or a student's kindness helps set a positive tone.

4. **Set Clear Expectations for Behavior:**

• Establish and communicate clear standards for respectful behavior in your environment (whether it is work, school, or family). Make sure everyone knows what is expected of them in terms of communication and interactions.

5. **Foster a Culture of Empathy**:

• Empathy helps people understand each other's perspectives, reducing the likelihood of conflict and promoting understanding.

6. **Offer Conflict Resolution Training:**

• If applicable, implement training videos about how to handle disagreements respectfully. That can include learning how to listen actively, how to express concerns constructively, and how to resolve conflicts without resorting to hostility.

7. **Encourage Cooperation Over Competition:**

• Establish a collaborative vision for success, especially in environments like workplaces or schools, fostering a cooperative spirit can lead to better teamwork, less conflict, and a stronger sense of community.

8. **Create Inclusive Spaces:**

• Make sure everyone feels heard and respected. Include diverse perspectives and make sure no one feels excluded or marginalized.

How to Manage Civility and Incivility in Student Athletes

1. **Game Day Behavior:**

• Before each game or season, set clear expectations for behavior both on and off the field or the court. Let athletes know what kinds of actions are considered inappropriate, such as taunting opponents, using foul language, or showing frustration in a disruptive manner.

• Remind athletes their behavior reflects not just on themselves but also on their teammates, their coaches, and the club.

2. **Encourage Emotional Regulation:**

• Help athletes develop skills for managing emotions during high-pressure situations. Competitive sports can provoke frustration, anger, and disappointment, but it is important athletes learn how to channel those emotions in a positive way.

• Teach simple coping techniques, like taking a few deep breaths, stepping back from a heated moment, or counting to ten when they feel anger or frustration rising.

3. **Address Incivility Immediately:**

• If a young athlete displays incivility, such as disrespecting an opponent or arguing with a referee, it is important to address it immediately. Let them know such behavior is not acceptable and explain why it is detrimental to the team's morale and reputation.

• Use those moments as teaching opportunities. Talk to the athlete privately to understand why they acted the way they did and guide them toward a more respectful response.

4. **Promote Accountability:**

• Help athletes take ownership of their actions. After an incident of incivility, have the athlete apologize to their teammates or opponent, if appropriate. That reinforces the idea their actions have consequences on others.

• Teach athletes to reflect on their behavior after a game or a practice. They can ask themselves questions like, "Did I treat my teammates and opponents with respect?" or "How could I have managed that situation better?"

5. **Use Consequences to Reinforce Expectations:**

• If an athlete continues to display incivility, it might be necessary to implement consequences that help them understand the importance of maintaining good behavior. That can include sitting out part of the game, having a conversation with the coach or the parents, or taking a short time out to reflect on their actions.

• Ensure consequences are consistent and fair, but always designed to be a teaching moment rather than punishment.

6. **Involve Parents in the Process:**

• Coaches should involve parents in conversations if an athlete's behavior becomes a recurring problem. Together, coaches and parents can help the athlete improve the athlete's behavior and provide guidance on how to manage emotions and pressure more effectively.

• Encourage open communication between parents, coaches, and athletes to create a supportive environment both on and off the field.

How to Manage Civility and Incivility

Here are specific examples and situations that can arise with student athletes and how to manage them with civility and incivility:

Example 1: Player Taunting after Scoring

Situation: After scoring a goal or making a great play, a young athlete taunts or mocks an opponent, either verbally or with gestures.

Handling Civility:

• Coach's Role: The coach can intervene immediately by calling the player over and calmly explaining while it is great to be proud of their accomplishment, showing disrespect to others does not reflect well on their character.

• Teach Empathy: Say something like, "Imagine how you would feel if the roles were reversed. How would you want to be treated?" That approach encourages the player to reflect on their behavior.

• Positive Reinforcement: Praise the athlete for playing well, but remind them, "True champions respect their opponents, win or lose."

Handling Incivility:

• Address the Behavior Immediately: If the behavior happens in real-time, have the player apologize to the opponent and remind the team about the importance of sportsmanship.

• Consequences: If that behavior becomes a pattern, the athlete might have to sit out part of the game or participate in a team discussion about respect and sportsmanship.

Example 2: A Player Yells at a Teammate

Situation: A player becomes frustrated after a missed opportunity or a mistake, and instead of being supportive, they yell at a teammate for not passing or for making an error.

Handling Civility:

• Teach Positive Communication: Have discussions with the student athletes about how to communicate constructively. Instead of yelling, use encouraging language. For example, you can say, "Hey, it is okay. Let us focus on getting the next one together."

• Supportive Environment: Coaches and team leaders can regularly reinforce the importance of lifting each other up during tough moments. Remind athletes teamwork is key for success and everyone makes mistakes.

- Model Calmness: If a player sees coaches or older teammates remaining calm during stressful situations, they will be more likely to mirror that behavior.

Handling Incivility:

- Immediate Intervention: If an athlete lashes out at a teammate, the coach should stop the situation by taking both players aside. Remind them yelling at teammates creates a negative atmosphere and disrupts the team dynamic.

- Apology and Reflection: Encourage the player to apologize to the teammate and provide an opportunity for the player to reflect on how they could have managed the situation more respectfully.

Example 3: A Player Argues with the Referee

Situation: A young athlete disagrees with a referee's decision and argues, showing frustration or even disrespect toward the official.

Handling Civility:

- Teach Respect for Officials: Emphasize referees are part of the game and their role is to ensure fairness. Coaches should encourage athletes to remain calm and focus on their performance rather than on questionable calls.

- Model Sportsmanship: If the coach disagrees with a call, they should do so respectfully and calmly, showing it is impossible to express frustration without disrespect.

- Team Discussion: Hold a team meeting during which players discuss the importance of respecting referees and not letting bad calls affect their attitudes or their play.

Handling Incivility:

- Stop the Argument: If an athlete is engaging in an argument with the referee, the coach should step in and end the discussion immediately. That helps to set a precedent for how players should act when they disagree with referee officials.

- Encourage a Reflection Moment: After the game, have the athlete reflect on their actions and encourage them to understand how disrespecting referees can lead to penalties, or even worse, a reputation for poor sportsmanship.

- Corrective Action: Depending on the severity of the behavior, you can apply a consequence for the player like sitting out part of the next game or being benched for poor conduct.

Example 4: Player's Frustration At an Opponent

Situation: After a missed shot or a turnover, a player pushes or shoves an opponent in frustration.

Handling Civility:

•Instill Emotional Control: Teach athletes how to control their emotions and use that energy to refocus on their game. For example, you can say something like, "When you feel frustrated, take a deep breath and channel that into positive energy to help your team."

• Reinforce Positive Conflict Resolution: Show athletes how to manage mistakes with maturity. You can say to them, "Instead of getting upset, focus on your next move. Every athlete makes mistakes, but great athletes bounce back."

• Public Praise for Resilience: When players show resilience after a tough moment, praise them for their ability to stay calm and keep their focus.

Handling Incivility:

• Immediate Action: If an athlete uses physical aggression, the coach should immediately stop the play and speak to the athlete. Explain the consequences of using physical aggression in sports, and reinforce the idea violence is never acceptable.

• Apology: The player should apologize to the opponent for their aggressive behavior, and the coach should discuss the incident with the team to reinforce the message aggression does not belong in sports.

• Consequences: Depending on the severity of the situation, the athlete can face disciplinary actions, such as being benched for part of the game or receiving additional training concerning controlling emotions.

Example 5: Player Credit for a Team Effort

Situation: A player celebrated their performance by taking full credit for a team victory, neglecting to acknowledge the efforts of teammates.

Handling Civility:

• Encourage Humility: Athletes celebrate as a team, acknowledging the efforts of their teammates in achieving success. You can say something like, "We win as a team, and we lose as a team."

• Praise Team Contributions: After a victory, highlight how each player contributed. For example, you can say, "Great shot by [Player A], but [Player B] made an amazing pass to set that up."

- Foster Team Bonding: Athletes recognize and appreciate each other's strengths, which helps build a supportive team environment.

Handling Incivility:

- Address the Ego: If a player is consistently taking credit for the team's efforts, gently remind them teamwork is the key to success. You can tell them, "Great individual performance, but remember, it is the whole team that worked together to get this win."

- Teach Accountability: Talk to the player privately if that behavior becomes a pattern, emphasizing how important it is to give credit where it is due and to recognize everyone's contributions.

Post-Game Interviews

Do's:

• Be Polite and Respectful: Always thank the interviewer for the opportunity to speak. A polite greeting and a thank-you at the end leave a lasting positive impression.

• Stay Positive: Focus on positive aspects of the game, even if the outcome was not favorable. Avoid blaming the other players, the referee, or making excuses.

• Give Thoughtful, Concise Answers: Keep your answers clear and to the point. You do not need to ramble. Think before answering to ensure you are giving a thoughtful response.

• Acknowledge Team Effort: If you had a great game, make sure to highlight your team's collective effort. Praise your teammates and your coaches.

• Be Honest, but Diplomatic: If something went wrong, it is okay to acknowledge it, but do so diplomatically. Talk about what you can improve, not just what went wrong.

• Use Positive Body Language: Maintain eye contact, stand or sit up straight, and avoid crossing your arms. Look engaged and enthusiastic.

- Represent the Team: Remember you are not just speaking for yourself, but as a representative of the team, the coaches, and the school. Keep that in mind, and stay composed.

- Stay Focused on the Question: Stay on topic and answer the specific questions asked. If the reporter asks multiple questions, answer them one at a time.

Do's and Don'ts During Post-Game Interviews

Don'ts:

• Don't Be Negative: Avoid criticizing teammates, coaches, or referees. Complaints or negative remarks make you look unprofessional and can hurt team morale.

• Don't Use Inappropriate Language: Watch your language, avoid slang, cursing, or anything that could come off as unprofessional and can hurt team morale.

• Don't Get Defensive: If asked about a mistake or a tough loss, do not get defensive or hostile. Instead, stay calm and acknowledge where improvement is needed.

• Don't Overdo It with "I" Statements: While it is important to take credit for your effort. Use "we" when talking about team successes or challenges.

• Don't Ignore the Audience: Always address the interviewer directly, but remember the audience (viewers or fans) is listening. Your response should be understandable and respectful to them, as well.

• Don't Rush Through the Interview: Take your time. Do not seem like you are in a hurry or eager to leave. Even after the interview is over, a polite handshake and a thank-you go a long way.

- Don't Over-Promise: Be careful with what you commit to do. Do not promise to do something unless you are sure you can follow through.

Sharing Interview Etiquette with Team

• Mock Interviews: There are online etiquette and manners videos available. Host mock interview sessions during practice so players can get used to talking to reporters and answering questions in a professional way. That will build their confidence.

• Provide Role Models: Highlight positive examples of professional athletes or individuals within the community who manage interviews well. That will show the team members how staying calm under pressure and speaking respectfully can set a good precedent.

• Emphasize Team-First Attitude: Reinforce interviews should emphasize the collective effort of the team over individual performance. That promotes humility and a dedicated team culture.

Incorporating those activities can help foster a sense of unity, civility, and good sportsmanship among coaching staff and student athletes. The key is to emphasize sportsmanship is not just about what happens during a game, but it is also about building lasting, supportive relationships both on and off the field or the court.

Wishing You All the Best!

Code of Conduct Definitions

Civility:

Civility is the act of showing respect for others by being polite, like the *civility* you showed in speaking kindly to someone who has hurt your feelings.

Etiquette:

Like manners, etiquette is a code of polite conduct. If you practice proper *etiquette*, you are less likely to offend or annoy people, and you might even charm them.

Incivility:

Incivility is being rude or disrespectful. A child will be scolded for his *incivility* if he sits with his elbows planted on the dinner table and is talking too loudly with his mouth full of food.

Manners:

Manners are the proper and the polite the way to behave in public. If you take your chewing gum out of your mouth and stick it on the table before a meal, you need to work on your *manners*. Manners vary in diverse cultures.

Sportsmanship:

Sportsmanship is a type of fairness expected of athletes. If you never cheat or act rudely while playing a game, you are modeling good *sportsmanship*. Sportsmanship has to do with how people play games, not if they win or lose them.

Resources:

Vocabulary.com. (n.d.). Civility. In *Vocabulary.com Dictionary*. Retrieved February 20, 2025, from https://vocabulary.com/dictionary/civility

Vocabulary.com. (n.d.). Etiquette. In *Vocabulary.com Dictionary*. Retrieved February 20, 2025, from https://vocabulary.com/dictionary/etiquette

Vocabulary.com. n.d.). Incivility. In Vocabulary.com Dictionary. Retrieved February 20, 2025, from https://vocabulary.com/dictionary/incivility

Vocabulary.com. (n.d.). Manners. *In Vocabulary.com Dictionary*. Retrieved February 20, 2025, from https://vocabulary.com/dictionary/manners

Vocabulary.com. (n.d.) Sportsmanship. *In Vocabulary.com Dictionary*. Retrieved February 2, 2025, from https://vocubulary.com/dictionary/sportsmanship

Afterword

Student athletes who have read this book now have a clearer understanding of the distinctions between civility, incivility, and sportsmanship.

You are living in a world full of opportunities and challenges. Your journey in both life and sports will involve highs and lows. When faced with difficult situations, don't hesitate to seek guidance from an adult. Whether you agree or disagree with the discussion, always ensure your actions and decisions demonstrate respect for everyone involved. Take time to reflect on the choices you have made and consider if there was a better way to manage the situation. If you realize you were wrong, try to correct your mistake and move forward. From that, you will feel a sense of relief and growth. Every experience, even the challenging ones, presents an opportunity for growth. As you move forward, remember each of those moments help prepare you for adulthood.

Embrace the gift of life, and live it to the fullest. Let your goals and your passions shape the authentic version of yourself. Love who you are, and remember you are here for a purpose. Be a good sport and share the wisdom you have gained with your fellow athletes.

Wishing you success in all your future endeavors as the ultimate athlete and the ambassador of civility!

About the Author

Karen brings twenty-eight years of dedicated service in the criminal justice field.

She holds a Bachelor of Science in Justice Administration and a Master of Science in Criminal Justice, with academic interests focused on the development of effective after-school programs that support youth success. Her professional training includes certifications such as Save Our Youth and the Teen Confidence Academy through the Professional Woman Network (PWN), founded by Linda Eastman, a global organization of coaches, consultants, and authors.

Earlier in her career, Karen taught Your Manners Matter, a national civility-based eighteen-week curriculum developed by Cynthia Grosso, founder of the Charleston School of Protocol and Etiquette, at a local community center.

Soon after, Karen devoted her time to traveling with her daughter, Kendria, embracing the role of a "volleyball grandma" for several years while supporting not one, but two student-athletes. Drawing from her professional background and personal experience, she wrote the Student Athlete Success Guide to complete the work she began years ago—helping young athletes and their families navigate the path to success on and off the court.

Notes:

Notes:

Notes:

Notes: